# jim dine designs for
# A MIDSUMMER NIGHT'S DREAM

Introduction by Virginia Allen

Selected from the drawings and prints collection of The Museum of Modern Art
General editor William S. Lieberman

The Museum of Modern Art, New York

# INTRODUCTION

In March 1966 a new production of William Shakespeare's *A Midsummer Night's Dream* opened at the San Francisco Actor's Workshop to the mingled delight and dismay of audience and critics alike. It was certainly not the *Midsummer* to which most were accustomed. The Workshop's theatrical director, John Hancock, had joined forces with New York painter Jim Dine to spawn a bastard production of the play totally outside established tradition. Dine's avant-garde designs for costumes and sets plus Hancock's adventurous stage direction produced a dynamic piece of happening-inspired theater, which was subsequently presented at the Pittsburgh Playhouse and at New York's Theatre De Lys.

Dine's rainbow motif dominated the production design. A large patchwork crazy-quilt — half in brilliant colors, half in shades of gray — concealed the stage, which was framed by a rainbow proscenium arch painted in house enamel. At one end of the rainbow an old-fashioned Wurlitzer juke-box glowed neon colors and blared Mendelssohn's "Wedding March" at sticky points in the plot. Black plastic sheeting draped the back of the sparsely set stage. The actors' costumes provided the only color on-stage, several of them sporting rainbows in miniature: Oberon's "magic-making" right hand painted in parallel bands of color, and Puck's entire body horizontally striped in red, orange, yellow, green, and blue makeup. Like some affluent mods of today or the Bobbsey twins of days past, the two pairs of lovers wore matching costumes in complementary colors: Hermia and Lysander in green and red, Demetrius and Helena in blue and orange. Only the six workmen who performed *Pyramus and Thisbe* wore neutral, earth-colored garments.

Props and special effects were similarly dazzling. Puck, wearing artificial red peonies behind each ear, made a swinging entrance on an overstuffed red satin heart suspended from the flies. Bottom wore a magnificent Steiff-like ass's head, bedecked with long floppy eyelashes. The director used glow-in-the-dark animated puppets to represent Peaseblossom, Mustardseed, Cobweb, and Moth, and suffused the stage with black light to produce an aura of the supernatural. The play opened with two plague doctors wheeling a cart full of unfortunate victims down the center ramp. Hippolyta, confined in her bamboo "marriage cage" and wearing black body makeup and a leopard-skin bikini, looked more like a snarling savage than like Theseus' prospective queen.

In the fall of 1964 Dine and Hancock had toyed with the idea of staging a happening about the Civil War, using life-size cardboard cutouts of the Blue and Gray heroes. Their plans fell through, but at Hancock's invitation they met again early in 1966 in San Francisco to discuss the proposed new production of *A Midsummer Night's Dream.* After a brief consultation, Dine returned to New York to complete his sketches in just two weeks. These spontaneous and amusing drawings are annotated in the artist's "billboardese" to suggest fabrics, colors, and even construction methods. Dine directed that all colors be "brite," that Oberon's one-piece leotard over football shoulder pads fit "rather skin tite," and that the seamstress "suppress that waist!" on Lysander's period costume. Dine also advised her to consider it a triumph if Mustardseed's shel-lacked fur seed pod turned out to be "fairly repulsive." Paper swatches pasted to the drawings indicate the exact colors to be used, and collage elements torn from magazines and advertisements suggest fabrics ranging from Nauga-hyde to army camouflage. The sketch for the proscenium arch even boasts a Red Devil paint chart with appropriate rainbow colors circled.

Color is the unifying factor throughout these drawings. Whether juxtaposing chromatic variants in Philostrate's purple costume or pairing complementaries in the lovers' costumes, Dine achieves maximum strength from his rainbow scheme. His judicious use of black in the backdrop, in Theseus' robe, and in the main curtain adds a staccato contrast and underscores the duality of real world and fairy kingdom in the play.

Major artists have often indulged their fascination with the world of the performing arts. Notably Chagall, Picasso, and Kokoschka have designed sets and costumes for ballets, operas, and dramatic plays. Beginning in the late fifties, though, an entirely new kind of artist participation in the theater sprang up. From an initial impetus in New York, happenings began happening all over the United States. Pop and avant-garde artists contributed their new images to poke deadly serious fun at contemporary society's tin gods. The ground was broken by such young artists as Red Grooms, Claes Oldenburg, Robert Rauschenberg, Larry Rivers, and Dine, many of whose earliest efforts were performed at the Reuben Gallery in New York. Other artists have since rallied to the movement, often adapting environmental theater ideas to formal theater productions. David Hockney, for example, designed sets and costumes for the 1966 London production of *Ubu Roi,* and Robert Indiana designed the Minneapolis Center Opera Company's *The Mother of Us All* in early 1967. Dine utilized motifs from his own happenings in these designs for *A Midsummer Night's Dream.* Plastic sheeting was used extensively in New York happenings and, originally, in presentations by the Gutai group in Japan. The prototype for Puck's rainbow stripes may have been Dine's own painted features in *The Smiling Workman, The Vaudeville Show,* and *The Shining Bed.* Similarly, Oberon's costume design doubtless derived from the all-silver central figure in *The Car Crash.*

In a happening, the artist-participant is to a great extent his own writer, director, costume designer, and performer. He is limited only to the extent that his interaction with the other performers must "work" or "be effective," and he ascribes great value to the spontaneous and accidental. Despite his pioneering involvement in the happening movement as author and performer, Dine had not executed designs for formal theater prior to the *Midsummer* project. The transition from the happening's "unpredictable collage of successive situations and events," as Al Hansen has defined it, to the play's prescribed sequence of action is difficult at best. The artist's more fanciful conceptions sometimes must be tempered with the trouper's knowledge of what will work. An actor required to leap around the stage may find it difficult to do so when confined from neck to ankle in cardboard. Hence Snug's apron, however visually appropriate, had to go. Peter Quince's hammers and saws and Tom Snout's pots and pans banged around too much, and were likewise blue-penciled. Stylistically Dine's designs alternate between traditional and way out — Theseus' Russian greatcoat and the lovers' period costumes on the one hand, Philostrate's Superman suit and Titania's Wonder Woman costume on the other. As production co-ordinator, Hancock decided that the visual jolt of space-age costumery would most effectively underscore his own antitraditional interpretation of the play. Retaining Dine's colors, he altered the lovers' costumes to space suits and capes for the men, and belted mini-skirted tunics with rainbow target bras (originally slated for Titania's costume) for the women.

Some costume sketches evolved as conceived, with minimal modification. Puck's rainbow body makeup made him one of the most effectively costumed performers in the production. Philostrate survived the transition from drawing board to stage without alteration, and Oberon's silver lamé leotard evolved into a loose shroud of the same material.

Did Jim Dine's designs work? Certainly they are successful as drawings, but no conception for the stage can be judged apart from the context of the production. The critics at the performances in San Francisco, Pittsburgh, and New York were impressed, baffled, amused, and — critical. Hancock's interpretation was deliberately vulgar, unleashing ribald elements in action and dialogue long suppressed in orthodox fairy-tale productions; some people were not ready for such "sacrilege." Whether casting a strapping six-foot man as "fair" Helena, or giving "gentle" Hermia the temper of a fishwife, Hancock constantly made a mockery of the polite conventions that often stifle the play in a gossamer of spun sugar. Long considered innocuous enough to serve as the high-school-student's introduction to Shakespeare, *Midsummer* emerged instead as a rather peppery piece of writing. There is no question that Dine's irreverent, uninhibited designs were appropriate to this black comedy of anti-romantic love. The shock of pure color and modern costumes erased decades of clichés and plummeted Hancock's production into the world of hippies and happenings. Had Hermia been rechristened Baby Jane Holzer, and Demetrius yclept Batman, the audience would not have batted its collective eye.


Virginia Allen

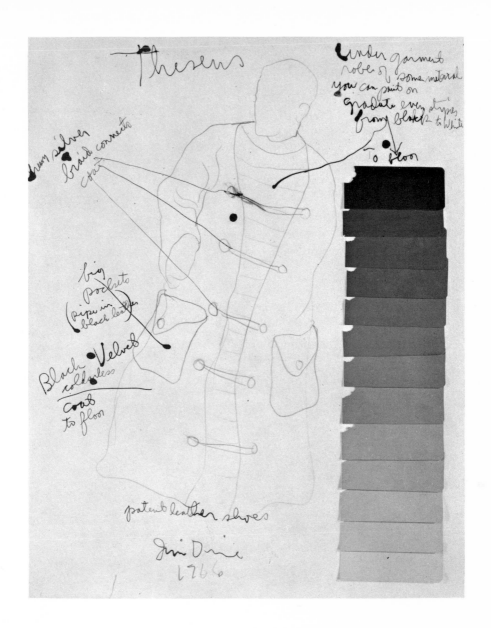

Theseus

under garment
robe of some material
you can print on
graduate every stripes
from black to White

dark silver
braid connects
coat

to floor

big
Pockets
(pipe in
black leather)

Black Velvet
collarless

coat
to floor

patent leather shoes

Jim Dine
1966

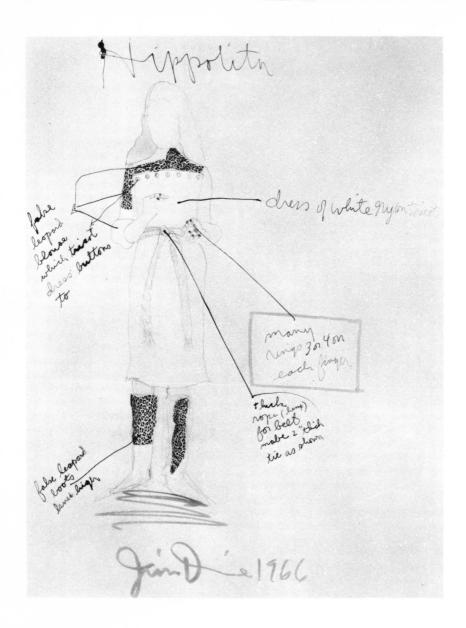

Hippolita

dress of white Nylon

false
leopard
blouse
which tiesst
dress buttons
to

many
rings 3 or 4 on
each finger

thick
rope (hemp)
for belt
make 2" thick
tie as shown

false leopard
boots
knee high

Jim Dine 1966

*Hippolyta, I woo'd thee with my sword,*
*And won thy love, doing thee injuries;*
*But I will wed thee in another key,*
*With pomp, with triumph, and with revelling.*

Act I, scene I

11

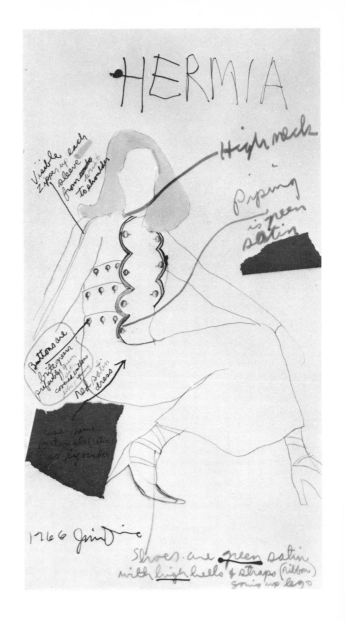

*The course of true love never did run smooth.*     Act I, scene I

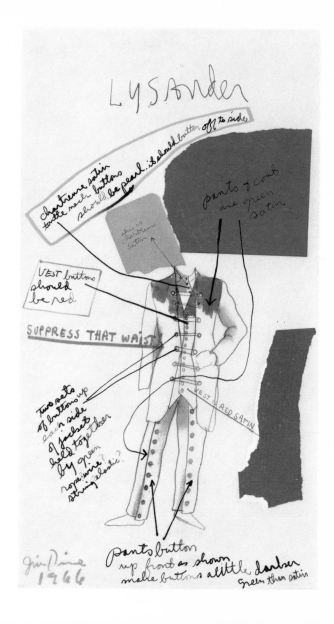

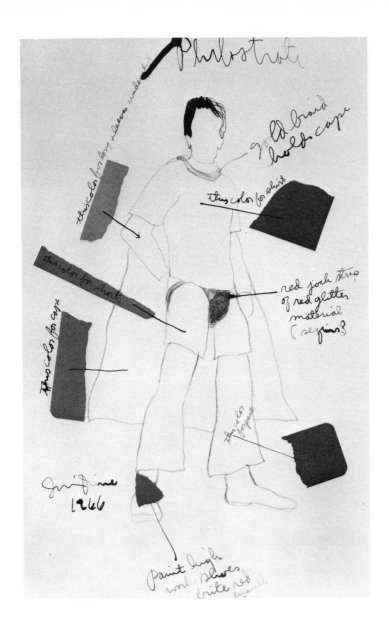

Philostrate

gold braid
holds cape

this color for long sleeve undershirt

this color for shirt

this color for shorts

red jock strap
of red glitter
material
(sequins?)

this color for cape

this color for puppets

June Jones
1946

paint high
wool shoes
brite red
enamel

14

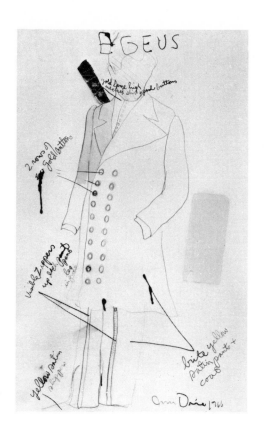

EGEUS

2 rows of *gold buttons*

invisible zippers up side of pant in leg

yellow satin zipper

brite yellow satin pants + coat

gold orange high neckties shirt + gold buttons

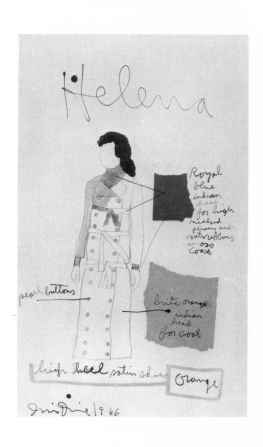

Helena

Royal blue indian head for high necked jersey und color ribbons across coat

pearl buttons

brite orange indian head for coat

high heel satin shoes    Orange

# PUCK

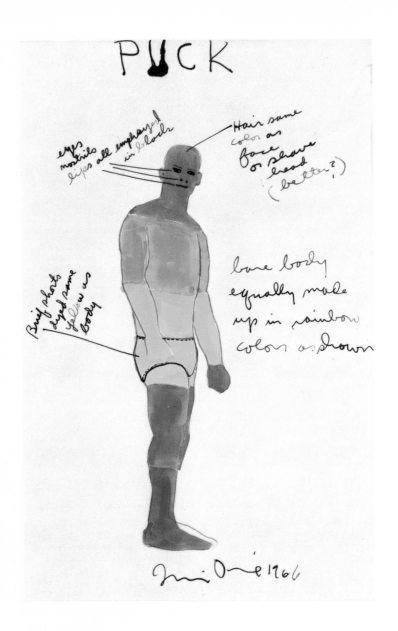

eyes nostrils lips all emphasized in black

Hair same color as face or shave head (better?)

Brief shorts dyed same yellow as body

bare body equally make up in rainbow colors as shown

*Lord, what fools these mortals be!*     Act III, scene II

OBERON, to PUCK

*Fetch me that flower; the herb I shew'd thee once;*
*The juice of it on sleeping eye-lids laid*
*Will make or man or woman madly dote*
*Upon the next live creature that it sees.*

Act II, scene I

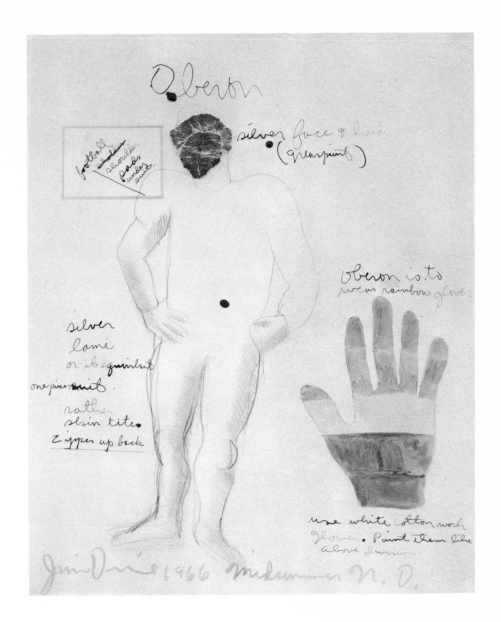

*Come, sit thee down upon this flowery bed,*
*While I thy amiable cheeks do coy,*
*And stick musk-roses in thy sleek smooth head,*
*And kiss thy fair large ears, my gentle joy.*

                                Act IV, scene I

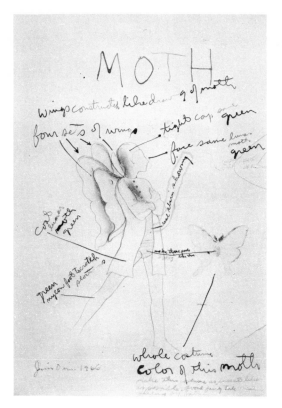

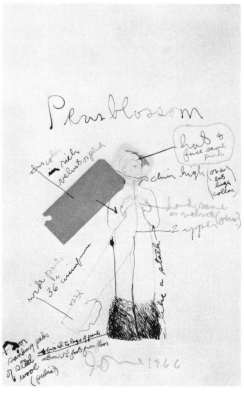

I'll give thee fairies to attend on thee:
And they shall fetch thee jewels from the deep,
And sing, while thou on pressed flowers dost sleep:
And I will purge thy mortal grossness so,
That thou shalt like an airy spirit go.
Peaseblossom! Cobweb! Moth! and Mustardseed!

Act III, scene I

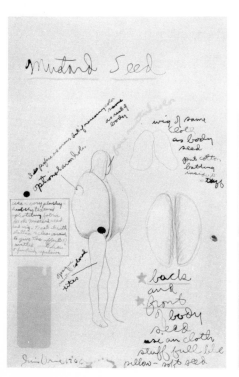

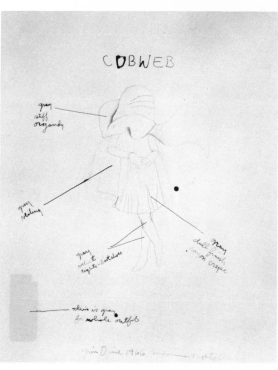

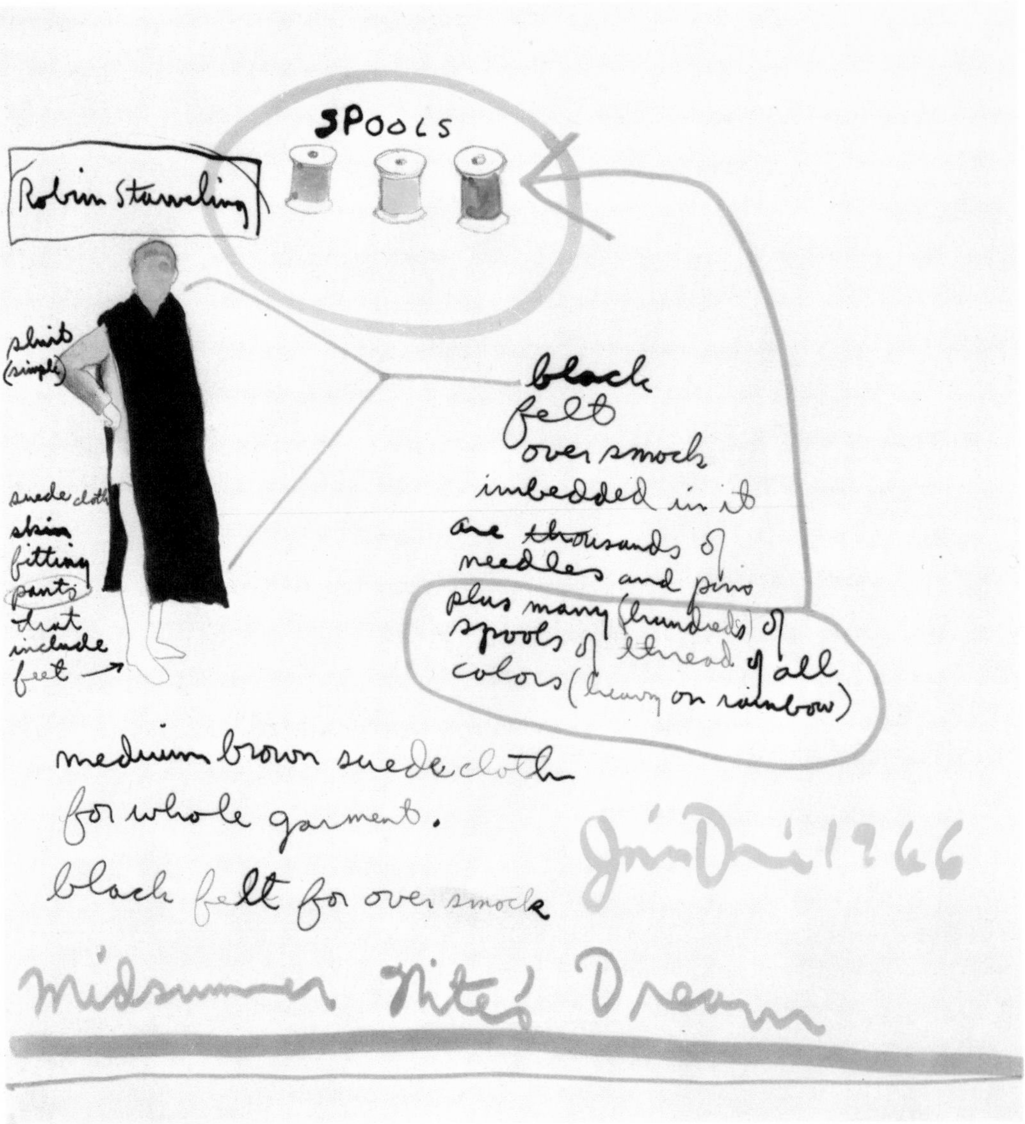

SPOOLS

Robin Starveling

shirt
(simple)

black
felt
over smock
imbedded in it
are thousands of
needles and pins
plus many (hundreds) of
spools of thread of all
colors (heavy on rainbow)

suede cloth
skin
fitting
pants
that
include
feet →

medium brown suede cloth
for whole garment.
black felt for over smock

Jim Dine 1966

Midsummer Nites Dream

24

THESEUS
*What are they that do play it?*
PHILOSTRATE
*Hard-handed men, that work in Athens here,*
*Which never labor'd in their minds till now;*
*And now have toil'd their unbreath'd memories*
*With this same play, against your nuptial.*

Act V, scene I

NICK BOTTOM

Pancho
cut
from
brown
tan
green
Camoflage
to
here

Pants of same
shoes of same

Jim Dine 1966

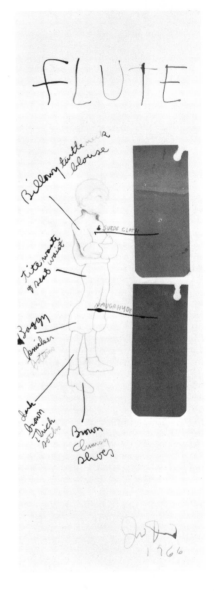

FLUTE

Billowy turtleneck blouse

SUEDE CLOTH

Tite waist
of real waist

NAUGAHYDE

Baggy
familiar
bottom

dark
brown
thick
socks

Brown
clumsy
shoes

Jim Dine
1966

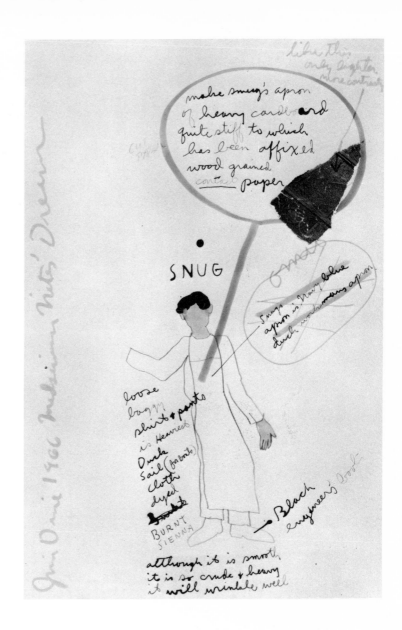

27

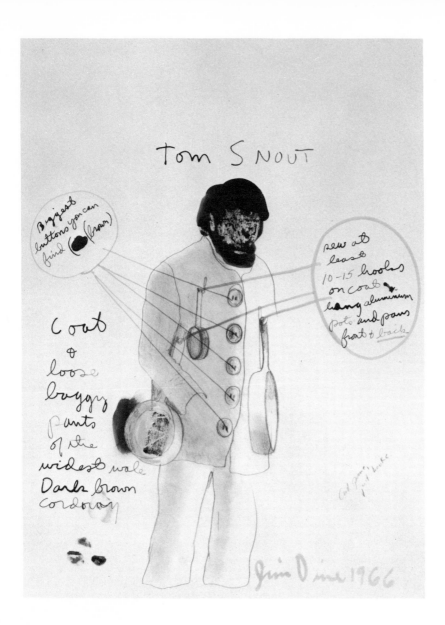

28

Peter Quince

SHIRT OF SAME TAN CANVAS

bare
bare
Chested

VEST OF
← NATURAL Colored
BURLAP (dark)
TAN
OR CANVAS

Many loops,
few tools

lots of
loop on
Vest & pants
to hold many
hammers, pliers
etc.
on both sides

← Pants that
billow
of natural colored
burlap (dark tan)

Shoe
boots
of
natural
burlap

try and line the clothes
with something like quilting to make burlap billow

*The iron tongue of midnight hath told twelve:*
*Lovers, to bed; 'tis almost fairy time.*
*I fear we shall out-sleep the coming morn,*
*As much as we this night have overwatch'd.*
*This palpable-gross play hath well beguiled*
*The heavy gait of night. Sweet friends, to bed.*
*A fortnight hold we this solemnity,*
*In nightly revels and new jollity.*

Exeunt

The following 32 costume and stage designs for *A Midsummer Night's Dream,* executed in February 1966, were given to the theater arts collection of The Museum of Modern Art, New York, by Mrs. Donald B. Straus, with the exception of numbers 23, 25, 26, and 27, gifts of the artist; 24, lent anonymously; and 22 and 28 lent by Nancy Dine. Measurements are of sheet size, in inches, height preceding width. Unless otherwise noted, all works are signed and dated, and are on tracing paper.

## COSTUME DESIGNS

### The Athenian Court

1. *Theseus.* Collage, pencil, pen and ink, 23⅞ x 19" (p. 9).
2. *Hippolyta.* Collage, felt pen, pencil, pen and ink, 23⅞ x 19" (p. 10).
3. *Philostrate.* Collage, glitter, felt pen, pencil, pen and ink, 19 x 12" (p. 14).
4. *Egeus.* Collage, felt pen, pencil, pen and ink, 19 x 12" (p. 15).
5. *Lysander.* Collage, felt pen, pencil, pen and ink, 17⅜ x 9½" (p. 13).
6. *Hermia.* Collage, felt pen, pencil, pen and ink, 19 x 10¼" (p. 12).
7. *Helena.* Collage, felt pen, pencil, brush, pen and ink, 19 x 13¾" (p. 15).

### The Fairy Kingdom

8. *Oberon.* Collage, felt pen, pencil, pen and ink, 23⅞ x 19" (p. 19).
9. *Titania.* Collage, crayon, glitter, felt pen, pencil, brush, pen and ink, 23⅞ x 19" (p. 21).
10. *Puck.* Felt pen, pencil, pen and ink, 14⅞ x 10" (p. 16).
11. *Moth.* Collage, crayon, felt pen, pencil, pen and ink, 16¾ x 11⅜" (p. 22).
12. *Peaseblossom.* Collage, felt pen, pencil, pen and ink, 19 x 12⅛" (p. 22).
13. *Mustardseed.* Collage, felt pen, pencil, pen and ink, 19 x 11⅞" (p. 23).
14. *Cobweb.* Collage, pencil, pen and ink, 23⅞ x 19" (p. 23).

### The Menials

15. *Nick Bottom (I).* Collage, crayon, felt pen, pencil, brush, pen and ink, 12 x 6⅛" (p. 26).

16. *Nick Bottom (II).* Collage, pencil, pen and ink, 17½ x 9½".
17. *Francis Flute.* Collage, pencil, pen and ink, 19 x 6½" (p. 26).
18. *Snug.* Collage, felt pen, pencil, brush, pen and ink, 19 x 12" (p. 27).
19. *Tom Snout.* Collage, metallic paint, crayon, felt pen, pencil, brush, pen and ink, 19 x 12" (p. 28).
20. *Peter Quince.* Crayon, felt pen, pencil, brush, pen and ink, 13 x 12" (p. 29).
21. *Robin Starveling.* Crayon, felt pen, pencil, brush, pen and ink, 12¾ x 11⅞" (p. 24).

## STAGE DESIGNS

22. *Proscenium Arch.* Collage, felt pen, pencil on paper, 24 x 36¼" (detail, cover).
23. *Main Curtain.* Felt pen, pencil, brush and ink, 19 x 23¾" (detail, end leaves).
24. *Side Curtain.* Felt pen, pencil, 19 x 23⅞".
25. *Heart.* (Not signed or dated). Felt pen, pencil, 19 x 23⅞".
26. *Moons.* (Not signed or dated). Felt pen, pencil, 19 x 11¹⁵⁄₁₆".
27. *Trees.* (Not signed or dated). Felt pen on paper, 24 x 36¼".
28. *Chandelier.* Crayon, felt pen, pencil, 18⅞ x 23⅞".

## REJECTED COSTUME DESIGNS

29. *Theseus.* Felt pen, pencil, brush, pen and ink, 14½ x 12".
30. *Philostrate.* Collage, felt pen, pencil, pen and ink, 11⅞ x 9½".
31. *Egeus.* Felt pen, pencil, pen and ink, 12 x 9½".
32. *Helena and Demetrius.* Collage, felt pen, pencil, pen and ink, 19 x 12".

*Photographs:* Guild Photographers, pp. 18, 20, 25, 30. Baron Wolman, pp. 11, 17. Malcolm Varon, color illustrations throughout. All other illustrations, Edward Peterson.